POWERFUL PREDATORS

FIERCE FISH

BookLife PUBLISHING

©2023
BookLife Publishing Ltd.
King's Lynn, Norfolk
PE30 4LS, UK

All rights reserved.
Printed in China.

A catalogue record for this book is available from the British Library.

ISBN: 978-1-80505-012-4

Written by:
Mignonne Gunasekara
Adapted by:
Charis Mather
Edited by:
Rebecca Phillips-Bartlett
Designed by:
Drue Rintoul

MIX
Paper from responsible sources
FSC® C113515

All facts, statistics, web addresses and URLs in this book were verified as valid and accurate at time of writing. No responsibility for any changes to external websites or references can be accepted by either the author or publisher.

AN INTRODUCTION TO BOOKLIFE RAPID READERS...

Packed full of gripping topics and twisted tales, BookLife Rapid Readers are perfect for older children looking to propel their reading up to top speed. With three levels based on our planet's fastest animals, children will be able to find the perfect point from which to accelerate their reading journey. From the spooky to the silly, these roaring reads will turn every child at every reading level into a prolific page-turner!

CHEETAH
The fastest animals on land, cheetahs will be taking their first strides as they race to top speed.

MARLIN
The fastest animals under water, marlins will be blasting through their journey.

FALCON
The fastest animals in the air, falcons will be flying at top speed as they tear through the skies.

PHOTO CREDITS

IMAGES ARE COURTESY OF SHUTTERSTOCK.COM. WITH THANKS TO GETTY IMAGES, THINKSTOCK PHOTO AND ISTOCKPHOTO.
RECURRING – AMOVITANIA. COVER – BRAINGRAPH. 4–5 – ALESSANDRO DE MADDALENA, DEGROOTESTOCK. 6–7 – RAMON CARRETERO, SERGEY URYADNIKOV. 8–9 – RICH CAREY, AQUABLUEDREAMS. 10–11 – KUDLA, OLEKSANDR (ALEX) ZAKLETSKY, CC BY 4.0, VIA WIKIMEDIA COMMONS. 12–13 – MIKHAILSH, RICH CAREY. 14–15 – ATHAPET PIRUKSA, FORMOSANFISH. 16–17 – HAYATI KAYHAN, GUENTERMANAUS. 18–19 – BLUE-SEA.CZ, ANDRIY NEKRASOV. 20–21 – FRANCESCO_RICCIARDI, SASCHA JANSON. 22–23 – MARTIN PROCHAZKACZ, ALTRENDO IMAGES.

CONTENTS

PAGE 4	Welcome to the World of Predators
PAGE 6	Worrying Great White Sharks
PAGE 8	Brutal Great Barracudas
PAGE 10	Extreme Electric Eels
PAGE 12	Ruthless Red Lionfish
PAGE 14	Strange Blotched Snakeheads
PAGE 16	Painful Red-bellied Piranhas
PAGE 18	Scary Reef Stonefish
PAGE 20	Sneaky Striped Anglerfish
PAGE 22	Fierce and Frightening
PAGE 24	Glossary and Index

Words that look like <u>this</u> are explained in the glossary on page 24.

WELCOME to the World of PREDATORS

The world is full of predators. Predators are animals that hunt other animals for food. To their prey, predators are terrifying!

Come along as we dive into the underwater world of predators.

Are you ready to meet some fierce fish?

WORRYING Great White SHARKS

Great white sharks are the biggest predator fish out there. They can grow up to around six metres long.

Great whites use their strong sense of smell to hunt.

They have powerful tails and hundreds of sharp teeth.

Brutal Great BARRACUDAS

At around two metres long, great barracudas are a scary sight. They have a long lower jaw that sticks out.

Great barracudas hunt by surprising their prey. They swim up quickly and snap them up in their sharp teeth.

EXTREME ELECTRIC EELS

Electric eels can make <u>electricity</u> in their bodies. They use it to <u>stun</u> their prey while hunting.

Their shocks can even hurt very large animals. Many predators know not to mess with these dangerous eels.

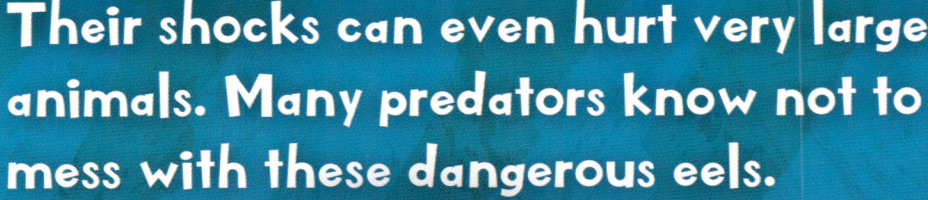

Ruthless Red LIONFISH

Red lionfish have <u>venomous</u> spines on their fins. These spines protect them from predators. The stings can be very painful.

When they hunt, red lionfish sometimes use their fins to stop their prey from escaping. Then, they swallow them whole.

STRANGE Blotched SNAKEHEADS

Most fish cannot breathe out of water. However, blotched snakeheads can.

This means they can make short trips over land.

Instead of chasing their prey, blotched snakeheads wait for their prey to come near them. Then, they attack suddenly.

PAINFUL Red-Bellied PIRANHAS

Sometimes, red-bellied piranhas get their food by scavenging.

Scavenging means eating dead plants and animals that they find.

Piranhas hunt live prey, too.

They have amazing hearing, which helps them find prey. Their teeth are sharp and triangular.

SCARY Reef STONEFISH

Reef stonefish are perfectly <u>camouflaged</u> against the sea floor.

They have venomous spines that keep them safe from other predators.

Reef stonefish sit very still and wait for their prey to come near. Then, they suck them in quickly.

SNEAKY Striped ANGLERFISH

Striped anglerfish have a body part that looks like a worm. This is called a lure.

LURE

If a striped anglerfish sits still and wiggles its lure, prey may come to see it. Prey are quickly sucked up.

FIERCE and FRIGHTENING

Predators come in many shapes and sizes. Thanks to their weapons and strength, there are some terribly fierce fish out there.

Some have sharp teeth or venomous spines. Some suck prey in whole.

These powerful predators are not to be messed with!

GLOSSARY

CAMOUFLAGED hidden by blending in with the surroundings

ELECTRICITY a powerful type of energy that can cause a painful shock

PREY animals that are hunted by other animals for food

STUN to shock in a way that causes someone to be unable to react

VENOMOUS able to poison another animal or person through a bite or sting

INDEX

ELECTRICITY 10
FINS 12–13
LURES 20–21
PLANTS 16
SPINES 12, 18, 23

TAILS 7
TEETH 7, 9, 17, 23